WITHDRAWN FROM
THE LIBRARY

UNIVERSITY OF
WINCHESTER

T

Ac

D1341863

KA 0186712 1

Just Like the Resurrection

By the same author

LOSS OF THE MAGYAR

THE SURVIVORS

Just Like the Resurrection

Patricia Beer

LONDON
MACMILLAN
MELBOURNE·TORONTO
1967

© Patricia Beer 1967

MACMILLAN AND COMPANY LIMITED
Little Essex Street London WC2
also Bombay Calcutta Madras Melbourne

THE MACMILLAN COMPANY OF CANADA LIMITED
70 Bond Street Toronto 2

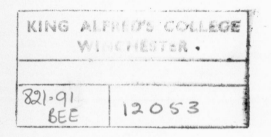

KING ALFRED'S COLLEGE
WINCHESTER .

821·91
BEE

12053

PRINTED IN GREAT BRITAIN BY
THE BOWERING PRESS PLYMOUTH

for Damien

Grateful acknowledgments are made to the following periodicals in which some of these poems first appeared: *London Magazine*; *Encounter*; *New Statesman*; *Listener*; *The Compleat Imbiber*, 1962; *New Poems* (P.E.N.), 1962; also to the Cheltenham Festival Programme 1966.

PB

Contents

The Postilion has been Struck by Lightning

He was the best postilion
I ever had. That summer in Europe
Came and went
In striding thunder-rain.
His tasselled shoulders bore up
More bad days than he could count
Till he entered his last storm in the mountains.

You to whom a postilion
Means only a cocked hat in a museum
Or a light
Anecdote, pity this one
Burnt at milord's expense far from home
Having seen every sight
But never anyone struck by lightning.

Overseas Student

This year they have set us
Lady into Fox.
I know what a lady is,
Smell, timbre and sex,
But not the other word,
It does not exist here.
So far I have not dared
To open the book. Fear
Of what the lady faces
Is better in ignorance.
If she goes into tight-laces
Or falls into a trance,
It would be quite harmless,
But in this huge hot land
Where so much is formless
I feel I cannot stand
Reading of some machine
That sucks her in perhaps,
Some angel she becomes, some queen.
Possibly two strong lips
Will take her, but will she then
Be in the stomach or the heart
Of a heroic man?
Shall I ever be able to start?

Lemmings

Lemmings die every year. Over the cliff
They pour, hot blood into cold sea,
So that you half imagine steam
Will rise. They do not part company
At first, but spread out, a brown team
Like seaweed, undulant and tough.

Light changes, and the wind may veer
As they swim out and on. The sea
May become sleek or shrewish. Foam
May blind them or may let them see
The wet horizon. It takes time.
They do not die within an hour.

One by one they leave the air
And drown as individuals.
From minute to minute they blink out
Like aeroplanes or stars or gulls
Whose vanishing is never caught.
All in time will disappear.

And though their vitality
Does not look morbid enough
People call it suicide
Which it has some appearance of.
But it may well be that the mood
In which each year these lemmings die

Is nothing worse than restlessness,
The need to change and nothing else.
They have learnt this piece of strand
So thoroughly it now seems false.
They jump, thinking there is land
Beyond them, as indeed there is.

On the Cobb at Lyme Regis

Here no one wins because no one contends.
The white wall curves, wheels, skating out to France,
And I walk on it, between warm water
And cold, little boats and leviathans.

Dangerous the sea is; for all I know
It is even now, underneath the skin,
Battering the sea-wall with drowned sailors
Or countrymen who carelessly fell in.

But there is no Poseidon any more
To rise with a seventh wave and thunder,
To turn on all taps and overwhelm me
Gone suddenly shapeless like a spider.

If I had magic to keep the sea down
I would feel exceedingly complacent
And walk the wall like Nelson at Port-Royal
Conscious of skill to blunt any trident.

But this safety is different. I know
From my teachers what is impossible.
I am in no danger, the sea cannot rise,
Which is the most frightening thing of all.

Scratch-path

Usually a scratch is a flaw
That would make a rosewood desk cheap
Or spoil a forehead for three days.

But computers depend on them.
Only through a scratch-path can they
Remember, and go the same way

Again. And even spongy brains
Live principally on scratches,
That make wood and skin suffer so.

Four Years After

'The perfectly preserved body of a British mountaineer was found near Courmayeur yesterday more than four years after he fell to his death on the Géant glacier.'

Yes, this was my husband, I
Cannot say 'is' though he has
Not changed since his dying day
Four years ago. Certainly
Ice is strong as saintliness
To keep corruption away.

I have altered in these years,
Better or less rightly wed,
Uglier or handsomer
Than I was then. All my tears
Rolled, grief like cargo shifted,
Grew and was cut like my hair.

I have moved but he not once,
For fifty moons not one cell.
Look at his glassy aplomb
Which has not been splintered since
Out of death and life he fell
To nothing. I could kill him.

Brunhild

My father laid me in a ring
Of fire, and then like thunder rolled
Away, though I had been more close
To him than in his arms. He told
Me I should never see his face
Now he had voiced me like a song,

Made me a separate thing, no more
His warrior daughter but a woman.
But I do see his face, I see
It all the time. Though I am human
He can still rule. He promised me
That a brave man should break the fire,

A man he would approve of, no
Tentative weakling. He will have
My father's dominant beard and mighty
Shoulders, and instead of love
This obligation to be doughty.
I wait for the entrance of the hero

Dressed up in my father's fashion.
If I were free to love I would
Decide on someone thin and shaven.
But in the ring I lie like wood
Or soil, that cannot yield or even
Be raped except with his permission.

Gallery Shepherds

Shepherds on old hills, with robber
And wolf lurking
Think themselves not so much seers
As hard-working.

But in paintings the mother of a god
Often blesses
Those who tend wool bodies topped
By wasp faces

And indeed shepherds are mostly shown
Simple and wise
In pictures, finding out things
Before spies.

Primed they come in from the country
To a small town
Thinking it glorious Gomorrah
That will burn.

Angels have spoken of a marvel
For countrymen
Who are portrayed as if gaping
At a con man.

The town needs them; they are followed
By knowing rich
Kings, entirely urban, whom the artist
Paints as such.

The Clock

The oldest clock we have
Stops every few days.
The weights catch on the case
And do not go right down.

It has the appearance
Of any eight-day clock.
We respect its size, not
Winding it like a watch.

The relative who gave
It to us used to say
A stopped clock foretells death,
Not thinking us so rash.

We have refuted this
Already, but it is
So easy to hear death
In the silence of stairs

Where once a pendulum
Thudded like a cart-horse
That now a deep meadow
Has swallowed, you can see

How some poets, like Donne,
Have 'used themselves in jest
By feigned deaths to die',
A run-through for the dark,

A drill. Obviously
Death cannot come each time
The clock stops. It may be
Good practice to think so.

Lion Hunts

A lion is never a lion in a royal hunt,
Only a victory to cheer the king up.
Sometimes six men carry him upside down,
His tail stiff as a leg, though his dewlap
Must be soft still because they grasp it.
He started proudly and knew when to stop.

Sometimes he stands, shoulder high to the king,
Nearly as good as the king, almost man to man.
Only his bare genitals and the ten weapons
Growing out of his paws show he is not one.
More honour to the king who is about to kill him.
A little of the blade has already gone in.

Years later he is in colour, so is the king
And they fight among pink rocks. A prince lies
Restfully dead, a cub watches to learn.
Magenta blood spurts from the lion's thighs
And the king's, but the curved sword is itching.
It must always be the animal who dies.

Pardoner's Tale Blues

I am Death, all bone and hair
   Mother, let me in
Get no health from this country air
   Mother, let me in.

What shall I do till Death can die?
What shall I do till he lies down
Till he lies down with his eyes at rest?
What shall I do till he dies?

Yes, God made me to live forever
   Mother, let me in
No deep earth and no deep river
   Mother, let me in.

Well run along men, to your bag of gold
   Mother, let me in
I cannot laugh, I am too old
   Mother, let me in.

And I knock upon the ground with my staff
   Mother, let me in
I can joke though I cannot laugh
   Mother, let me in.

Leaping into the Gulf

Children do not ask the proper questions
Of themselves, or so they come to think
Long afterwards. I do not feel I should
Have wondered who Curtius was, and why
He leaped and with what consequences.
Laziness and knowing that a painting
Was not a history lesson, absolved me then,
Forgive me now. But why did I not say:

A man who holds his shield up against nothing
Is mad, surely? A man who drops the reins
As though a horse needs no guidance through air
Has no sense of responsibility.
A horse that puts its head down, its behind up,
Like a dog trying to look harmless,
Can it be desperate? Should the hero wear
The artist's face without his spectacles?

A glare on paint was all I really saw,
Something inside a frame to goggle at,
A work of art. I certainly never laughed
At Haydon, as I hear so many did.
I simply stood there, well-grown for my age,
Bandaged and blindfolded and gagged,
Near a gulf, too, but very far from leaping.
I would as soon have answered my mother back.

The Return of the Prodigal

The point of no return
Would have been easier to fix
Perhaps than the moment

When I decided to leave the house
Where the lovers cried like peacocks
If they were not too drunk,

Where men urinated all over the place,
Where the pigs ate disgusting messes
And the dog almost nothing.

Certainly there was a point in time
When I put one bandaged leg forward,
Jolting the sores, and bent

The other leg with the bare knee,
Ready to walk to the gate, to shift
The cow lying across it

And start on the journey home.
I did so. I remember doing so.
But the decision took place

Either yesterday or this morning
As I was thinking it all over
Some fifty years later.

Poets' Corner

Here I come, the poet Drayton,
Quite convinced of my salvation

Through the death of Christ the Son,
In the year sixteen thirty one,

But not convinced of fitting honour.
In heaven there is no poets' corner,

Only sinners saved by grace.
I may not get a special place.

I put my earthly laurel down
And reach out for a heavenly crown.

O God, who art creative too,
Recognise me, give me my due,

And now my wordly leaves have faded
Let me not remain bareheaded.

Armistice Day

As I was going to work that morning
I saw the flag at half mast
And remembered individual death,
A young cousin who choked, a grandfather
Who rattled all night like snoring
And several others.

I did not ask for some time
'Who?'
Being afraid to know
To hear someone's name.

It was Armistice Day
So I was finally told.

Why ever did I say: 'What a relief,
I thought somebody was dead.'
For I remember plural death
As well as singular,
The red mutilated sky over Plymouth
And in the moorland towns
The ambulance men standing by all night
And several other incidents.

Head of a Snowdrop

After the north-east wind I carried
A snowdrop indoors. Taut as a bead
And bright, it lay in a bottle-top,
Nothing but petal from the wound up.

Its roots, stem, were still out of doors; strange
That away from them it could so change,
Normally opening into flower,
Wide as a primrose in one warm hour.

Human fingernails and hair move less
After death and lack naturalness.
Births after death — young Macduff — have such
Horror they can be used by a witch.

Anti-vivisectionists show men
Keeping dogs' heads alive, yapping even.
Schoolboys studying the Stuarts laugh
About Charles talking with his head off.

And I have this freak on my own hearth
Making me think about roots and birth
By false analogies and ignore
Its fulfilled purpose: an open flower.

Concert at Long Melford Church

FOR JANE LOWENSTEIN

Long Melford church is built of flint and glass,
The tombstones make your teeth ache
And the paths leading up to it look
Particularly hard through so much soft grass.

Today a concert in afternoon light
Gives the church a more brittle purpose
Than usual, more capable of close.
From this people will go home free tonight.

And there are so many. A Suffolk Festival
Has brought everybody out from London
Like a saint or a marvel. The proportion
Of living men to graves is medieval.

We were taught not to walk on graves as children.
Holding flowers for grandparents, we worked out
Where each corpse would be, walked round it,
Steering past the heels, elbow and chin

Of those submerged and dangerous bodies.
But today the paths and the narrow porch
Cannot contain those coming out of church
During the interval, into the sun and yew trees.

They spread all over the churchyard. They scan
The crowd, recognise, smile and shake hands.
By each tombstone a well-dressed person stands.
It looks just like the Resurrection.

Christmas Carols

They say a maiden conceived
Without so much as a kiss
At the time or afterwards.
Gloria in excelsis.

They name the eternal hall
Where we arrive to wine, fire,
Together and loving, but
Dead. *Quam dulcis est amor.*

Although in their description
Every midnight is clear
So that angels can be seen
Without peering, *hilariter,*

We know better in our fear
And avoid most carefully
David's city after dark.
Honor tibi, Domine.

In a Country Museum

This is a strange museum. In one square yard see
A mummified ibis and a postilion's boot.
Grey litter fills the house. For years every dead man
Had some cast-off curious object to donate.

Mindless and slovenly it is, but in one room,
Close to five jars that once held Daffy's Elixir,
Lies something that takes shape. A pallid patchwork quilt
Wrapped in cellophane, is spread on a four-poster.

A card describes the maker, a fourteen-year-old
Servant girl, with no book-learning and no siblings,
Who saved up half-a-crown for the big central piece
Of cloth, and got up at dawn on summer mornings.

This sounds sober and worthy, but the card goes on
To say that, interviewed at eighty, Mrs. Brew
Declared it had given her much greater pleasure
Than anything in all her life. If it is true

That to labour on these plodding squares meant more
Than marriage bed, children and a belief in God,
It is the best country marvel in this building
And suitably placed among these bright fields of food.

Summer Song for me and my Aunts

Never forget the moors
Behind the house, never
Let being a woman
Or the baking of bread
Or sizing up a sermon

Keep you off the heath
And far from the stone wall
That is no more than gauze
To these strong winds.
Headaches come indoors.

Walk uphill from the house
And the graves already there.
The chill of waterfalls
Cannot cause worse coughing
Than sprig-papered walls

Where you die in turn
On a narrow sofa
Boxed up from the storm.
Dying women can walk
On the moors without harm.

The Chemist's Dream

When I started on my life's work
My early ambition was bold
To the point of naïveté.
It was to change things into gold,

To make meadows stiffer than corn
Twanging in the wind like a lyre,
To find rabbits in the last swath
Paralysed with gold not terror,

To make towns like missals painted
By lavish monks, a stiff-necked swan,
A gay witch melting in the fire,
Spinning tops brighter than Saturn.

Subtler I next looked for long life,
The elixir of never-die.
The tetchiness of old people
And their hairbreadth sleep bothered me.

I wanted to keep them clever,
To be relied on. I included
Myself in this discovery
But once again was evaded.

For I am poor and past my prime
And now the third part of my quest
Needles me, to find the liquid
That teachers call the alkahest.

It will dissolve everything
It comes in contact with, the noose,
The throne, lutes and battering rams,
It is power, easy to use.

It will create no such problems
As wealth and eternal life set,
Except one, what to keep it in.
Which I will solve when I find it.

Spell

When after many deeds the witch
Buried some bones in my back yard
To bring about my destruction
I could think at last, 'This is hard.'

She had cut a cock's throat at me
Already, but still I grew rich,
Healthy and important, because
I had guilt enough to match

And far more guilt than her first move
Had called for, wax image and pins.
That had been child's play, her evil
Less animated than my sins.

But this burying of bones is more
Than I deserve, two eyes awake
Against two sleeping, so near home,
Such strong gods against guilt so weak.

I speculate from fear: did she
Need a lantern? were the bones wrapped
In anything to be brought here?
Did worms grow restless where she stepped?

My innocence will be the death
Of me. I have lived too chastely
To shore up guilt against these bones.
I have not been killed honestly.

Young Widow

It is a luxury at my age
To say 'I am too old' when asked to marry.
Autumn leaves, fading coals and sunset
Are metaphors to state that I am weary

But no more than that; sunset does not
Become darkness, nor a live coal a dead one.
Perhaps I should have called in the stars
And proved that no one born under Scorpion

Can take up with a Crab. Class or race
Might have been good excuses, or heart scared
By sorrow. It is deft and polite to tell lies
To a suitor. The truth is, I am dead tired.

On Saturday evening I said no,
But on Sunday morning walked in bad weather,
My own mistress, around the churchyard
Where people older than I lay together.

The Baptism

Beloved daughter, you must be
Totally immersed. To douse
The fiend is not the purpose
But because it was once done
By a baptizer called John.
(No Saint, it would be popery,

We are all saints.) If the saints
Stare at your wet frock, let them.
Lust is locked up in a hymn.
I shall stare too. The body
Is a grand chain, even I
Invite my daughter to dance.

It is life to us, this mock death.
Out in the streets the dryness,
The no-water holds menace.
What dance-hall, what cinema
Could provide us with such drama
As taking a virgin's breath?

Afterwards we shall all read
Passages from the Bible
About breasts and the able
Bridegroom who does not dally,
Words which long since turned chilly
And static in my own bed.

I know you have never felt
What I and the brethren have.
This warm-water tank, this grave
Is quite tasteless to the sons
And daughters of Puritans.
They lose everything but guilt.

I have been white hot, have been
Out in blizzards of desire.
If you wake up to stale air
Thank God for this legacy:
I give you with love today
A sixth sense, the sense of sin.

Abbey Tomb

I told them not to ring the bells
The night the Vikings came
Out of the sea and passed us by.
The fog was thick as cream
And in the abbey we stood still
As if our breath might blare
Or pulses rattle if we once
Stopped staring at the door.

Through the walls and through the fog
We heard them passing by.
The deafer monks thanked God too soon
And later only I
Could catch the sound of prowling men
Still present in the hills
So everybody else agreed
To ring the abbey bells.

And even while the final clang
Still snored upon the air,
And while the ringers joked their way
Down round the spiral stair,
Before the spit of fervent prayer
Had dried into the stone
The raiders came back through the fog
And killed us one by one.

Father Abbot at the altar
Lay back with his knees
Doubled under him, caught napping
In the act of praise.
Brother John lay unresponsive
In the warming room.
The spiders came out for the heat
And then the rats for him.

Under the level of the sheep
Who graze here all the time
We lie now, under tourists' feet
Who in good weather come.
I told them not to ring the bells
But centuries of rain
And blustering have made their tombs
Look just as right as mine.

Foam: Cut to any Size

The shopkeeper of whom I know nothing
Except this notice and the hard threatening goods
Drawn up inside his tight window
Probably has no whimsy in him,
Certainly lives ten miles inland.

Whimsical myself, I would say
That to cut foam is not beyond the power
Of someone who keeps files, hammers,
Mangles and mowers, that can change the shape
Of wet clothes, grass and iron.

Of course I know what he means
But the words rattle my ancestors
Who all their lives fought against foam
Which finally jumped down their throats
And cut them, before the crabs could.

Postcard

Snow fell on London Zoo. The Polar bears
Turned grey in half an hour. Quickly they stopped
Looking at the North, for it came flying past.
They saw the cold for the first time in years,
Choosing and nosing one piece as it dropped,
One flake to them smelling of all the rest.

There are advantages in any prison.
Bears have more food here, more security,
Freedom to breed though not much wish to do so.
But now the air is visible and the season
Can be touched, now that they feel and see
Their white stone ledge upholstered into snow,

They sicken for the perils of their home.
We are all lucky perhaps to live away
From danger, to receive only a few
Random cold flakes of fear out of the storm
Massing somewhere else. Yet on a day
Like this, the only safety seems to be

In the great blizzard playing at the pole,
Where danger could become our native land,
The central place, inside this fringe of fear.
And every touch of snow seems to recall
Some light and menacing postcard from a friend,
'Having a lovely time. Wish you were here.'

The Devonshire House

Three men set out from Devonshire
To overtake a thief
In weather when the wind raised tears
Bigger than any grief
And had sealed up in winter cold
The smells of farm and leaf.

Out of their county climbed the men,
Snug still from the lanes,
And they grew tall upon the roads
As hedges sank to plains,
The road that all the rebels took,
Hanged long since for their pains.

A mile ahead the thief stepped out
Who should by rights be dead.
Remembering how he stole the ewe
He wore her fleece like lead
And wished he could turn back the wind
That blew him through the deed.

At last he reached a piping inn
Where every traveller stops.
Inside the guests were sitting round
As warm as mutton chops
While like a flame at chimney mouth
Ale darted through their lips.

But he passed by, his guilt as sharp
As the gravel in his shoe.
'Oh Lord', he said ,'I am a ghost,
I must be spoken to,
Before I can accost mankind
From whom I stole a ewe.'

Soon the pursuers found the inn.
They lifted their cold eyes
To where a board creaked at the owls,
And saw to their surprise
A sign that showed a thatched cottage
And said 'The Devonshire House.'

The first man cried 'The thief is here.
He is a Devonshire man.
Will he not go inside and get
Some comfort while he can?
That is what I would do myself.'
But this impressed no one.

The next man laughed and said 'You are
As simple as a snail.
Why would he risk his ticklish throat
By packing it with ale,
Knowing his train of thought was one
We could pursue as well?'

Then the third man started to smile
And thought and smiled again
Until the grin went round his face
Smug as a daisy chain.
(His wife had left him years ago
But he had a thinking brain.)

'The thief will start by arguing
Just as you say he has
But then conclude his being here
Is the last thing we should guess.
So we shall find the villain sat
Upon his crooked arse.'

Then they ransacked the Devonshire House,
The thief was not inside.
So on and on the three men trudged,
The thief trudged on ahead.
He had not reasoned as they thought
Because he could not read.

That night pursuers and pursued
All perished in the storm.
They lie now neither tired nor spry,
Neither cold nor warm,
And every argument on earth
Goes round and round with them.

A Dream of Hanging

He rang me up
In a dream,
My brother did.
He had been hanged
That morning,
Innocent,
And I had slept
Through the striking
Of the clock
While it had taken place,
Eight,
Just about time enough
For it to happen.
He spoke to me
On the telephone
That afternoon
To reassure me,
My dear brother
Who had killed nobody,
And I asked him,
Long distance,
What it had felt like
To be hanged.
'Oh, don't worry, lovey', he said,
'When your time comes.
It tickled rather.'

A Visit to Little Gidding

This is a place of departure
Not of arrival. Even the signpost
Saying Little Gidding, a shock
To any poetry-lover, seems
Meant to be read retrospectively
By tourists on their way back.

As we rise from the fens to where
The hills begin, the flatlands
Give the impression of leaving
Us rather than being left
And they carry the sun away on them,
Warmth going not cold coming.

The pilgrims have gone; they have been
Here this afternoon with flowers
For Ferrar's tomb, so large a wreath
They were either rich or numerous,
We do not know which, they have gone
And their flowers are bright and dying.

The Scouts camping in the next field
Are lugging tea-urns and dismantling
Trestle tables. It has been visitors'
Day, but the parents have gone
Now, leaving their stalwart sons
Jesting shakily like survivors.

And we must go, if we want to be home
Before dark, for home is not here,
Less here, in fact, than in most places.
We are visiting a famous poet
Who followed a famous king
Who sought out a famous good man

And so on back to the beginning,
Which is the end, where the line vanishes,
Where the mirrors stop reflecting.
And the prayers, the escape-route
And the poem were perhaps
Not light coming but darkness going.

The Best Province

I like it here. Soldiers, administrators
And wives all pull strings to be posted
Here in mid-empire, south of the cold.
I come of rather good family myself.

I like the biggest arenas to applaud in,
To walk beneath trees that are set as puddings
Except at evenings when they boil with pigeons,
To have a choice between sun and shadow.

I like these aqueducts that carry men
And chariots as well as water through the sky
Then let them run free through forests. These Gauls,
Some of them, are nice enough to be Romans.

I should emphatically not have liked
To fight bright blue men in the rain, to head
Letters 'Verulamium' or 'Uriconium'
And enclose proud explanations of failure.

It is not as if I could have made up for it
Afterwards, done well at Hadrian's wall, for instance,
And been sent here by way of promotion.
Some diseases bring permanent loss of balance.

Fellow citizens, get what you want the first time
Round. It is interesting to make a false start,
You could write a book about it or ten poems
But would be happier if you did not have to.

47

KING ALFRED'S COLLEGE
LIBRARY